Contents

EmnETT

KU-486-887

Finding and identifying mammals in Britain

G B Corbet

British Museum (Natural History)
London 1975

©Trustees of the British Museum (Natural History)
Publication number 775
ISBN 0 565 00775 0
BMNH/159/7m/6/75
Printed in Great Britain by Staples Printers Limited
at The George Press, Kettering Northamptonshire

Introduction

Some of the wild mammals of the British Isles, such as squirrels and rabbits, are familiar to anyone who takes the slightest interest in the countryside. But many more, even abundant and widespread ones like the pygmy shrew, the weasel or the bank vole, are seldom seen by the casual observer, and considerable expertise is required simply to detect their presence, let alone observe and study them. This book is intended to help the beginner acquire such expertise, with the emphasis on the techniques of initial detection and precise identification, rather than the more detailed study that may follow. It deals with all terrestrial mammals from mice to deer and including bats and seals, but not the entirely marine cetaceans, i.e. the whales and dolphins. These are dealt with in a separate booklet by F. C. Fraser (See p. 54). The reporting of stranded cetaceans plays a very important part in studying these animals and anyone finding a stranded animal or a skeleton is urged to notify the local coastguard officer as quickly as possible.

Finding mammals may be a preliminary to more detailed study of a particular species, but it also by itself makes an important contribution to any faunal survey such as is increasingly required as a basis for conservation of habitats. Such surveys may be of a small discrete area that is being proposed as a nature reserve; or they may be of a larger area such as a county, so that maps of local distribution can be prepared as a base line by which further changes in distribution can be monitored. Many local natural history societies and museums operate such programmes and on a national scale the Mammal Society, in collaboration with the Biological Records Centre of the Institute of Terrestrial Ecology, is collecting records and preparing maps for the whole country. Most operations of this kind welcome help from anyone interested, and some information about how you can contribute is given on p. 52.

What is there to find?

The diversity of mammals in the countryside of Great Britain and Ireland is greater than most people would guess, although by comparison with the continent of Europe our mammalian fauna is considerably depleted. Altogether there are about 60 different species in Great Britain (not counting the entirely marine whales and dolphins). In a typical, well-wooded area of southern England there are about 30 species for the diligent naturalist to track down, and it would be difficult to find a few square kilometres anywhere in the country with fewer than ten.

The following list includes all those species now living in a wild state in Great Britain, along with all vagrant bats and pinnipeds that have been recorded. It does not include species that have become extinct. In fact no native species has become extinct in Great Britain since the wolf was finally exterminated in the 18th century.

Checklist of mammal species in Great Britain and Ireland

Symbols indicating the areas of Great Britain to which the species is confined: ● widespread; N northern; S southern; W western; SW south-west; SE south-east.

Scientific name	Vernacular name	Gt. Britain	Ireland	Remarks
Order Marsupialia – marsupials				
Family Macropodidae				
Macropus rufogriseus	**Red-necked wallaby**	Local		Introduced
Order Insectivora – insectivores				
Family Erinaceidae				
Erinaceus europaeus	**Hedgehog**	●	●	
Family Talpidae				
Talpa europaea	**Mole**	●		
Family Soricidae				
Sorex araneus	**Common shrew**	●		
Sorex minutus	**Pygmy shrew**	●	●	
Neomys fodiens	**Water shrew**	●		
Crocidura russula	**Greater white-toothed shrew**			Guernsey, Alderney and Herm only
Crocidura suaveolens	**Lesser white-toothed shrew**			Jersey, Sark and Scilly Is. only
Order Chiroptera – bats				
Family Rhinolophidae				
Rhinolophus ferrumequinum	**Greater horseshoe bat**	SW		
Rhinolophus hipposideros	**Lesser horseshoe bat**	S	W	
Family Vespertilionidae				
Myotis mystacinus	**Whiskered bat**	S	●	
Myotis brandti	**Brandt's bat**	S		
Myotis nattereri	**Natterer's bat**	S	●	
Myotis bechsteini	**Bechstein's bat**	S		

Scientific name	Common name	Status	Notes
Myotis myotis	Mouse-eared bat		S. coast
Myotis blythi	Lesser mouse-eared bat		? Vagrant
Myotis daubentoni	Water bat	•	
Vespertilio murinus	Parti-coloured bat		Vagrant
Eptesicus serotinus	Serotine	S	
Nyctalus leisleri	Leisler's bat	S	
Nyctalus noctula	Noctule	S	
Pipistrellus pipistrellus	Pipistrelle	•	
Pipistrellus nathusii	Nathusius' pipistrelle		? Vagrant
Barbastella barbastellus	Barbastelle	S	
Plecotus auritus	Common long-eared bat	•	
Plecotus austriacus	Grey long-eared bat	S	
Order Lagomorpha – lagomorphs			
Family Leporidae			
Lepus capensis	Brown hare	•	Introduced
Lepus timidus	Mountain hare	N	
Oryctolagus cuniculus	Rabbit	•	Introduced
Order Rodentia – rodents			
Family Sciuridae			
Sciurus vulgaris	Red squirrel	•	
Sciurus carolinensis	Grey squirrel	•	Introduced
Family Cricetidae			
Clethrionomys glareolus	Bank vole	•	Introduced
Microtus agrestis	Field vole	•	
Microtus arvalis	Orkney and Guernsey vole	•	Orkney and Guernsey only ? Introduced
Arvicola terrestris	Water vole	•	

Scientific name	Vernacular name	Gt. Britain	Ireland	Remarks
Family Muridae				
Apodemus sylvaticus	Wood mouse	●	●	
Apodemus flavicollis	Yellow-necked mouse	S		
Micromys minutus	Harvest mouse	S		
Mus musculus	House mouse	●	●	Introduced
Rattus rattus	Ship rat (Black rat)	●	●	Introduced; confined to ports
Rattus norvegicus	Common rat (Brown rat)	●	●	Introduced
Family Gliridae				
Muscardinus avellanarius	Dormouse	S		
Glis glis	Fat dormouse	S		Introduced
Family Capromyidae				
Myocastor coypus	Coypu	SE		Introduced
Order Carnivora – carnivores				
Family Canidae				
Vulpes vulpes	Fox	●	●	
Family Mustelidae				
Martes martes	Pine marten	N & W	●	
Mustela erminea	Stoat	●	●	
Mustela nivalis	Weasel	●		
Mustela putorius	Polecat	Wales		
Mustela furo	Ferret	●		Feral
Mustela vison	Mink	●	●	Introduced
Meles meles	Badger	●	●	
Lutra lutra	Otter	●	●	
Family Felidae				
Felis silvestris	Wild cat	N		

Order Pinnipedia – pinnipedes				
Family Phocidae				
Halichoerus grypus	Grey seal	●		
Phoca vitulina	Common seal	●		
Phoca hispida	Ringed seal		Vagrant	
Pagophilus groenlandicus	Harp seal		Vagrant	
Erignathus barbatus	Bearded seal		Vagrant	
Cystophora cristata	Hooded seal		Vagrant	
Family Odobenidae				
Odobenus rosmarus	Walrus		Vagrant	
Order Artiodactyla – even-toed ungulates				
Family Cervidae				
Cervus elaphus	Red deer	●		
Cervus nippon	Sika deer	●		Introduced
Dama dama	Fallow deer	●		Introduced
Capreolus capreolus	Roe deer	●		
Muntiacus reevesi	Chinese muntjac		S	Introduced
Hydropotes inermis	Chinese water deer		S	Introduced
Family Bovidae				
Capra (domestic)	Goat	●		Feral

What further changes can we expect to see in the above list? In the first place it is quite conceivable that further exotic species will establish themselves. The latest colonist included in the list is the American mink which became firmly established outside captivity about 1957. More recently there have been reports of porcupines and racoons at large but it remains to be seen whether these will result in established breeding populations.

Two recent additions to the list of bats, Brandt's bat, *Myotis brandti* and the grey long-eared bat, *Plecotus austriacus,* were previously confused with closely related species, the whiskered bat, *M. mystacinus* and the common long-eared bat, *P. auritus.* It is possible, but increasingly unlikely, that further bats will prove to be pairs of closely similar 'sibling species'.

It is probable that most populations of small rodents and shrews on small islands such as the Channel Islands and the Hebrides owe their origin to accidental introduction by man. It is therefore possible that further island populations may come to light, perhaps involving continental species not yet recorded in Britain.

One recent addition to the list of bats, Nathusius' pipistrelle, is based on a find of a single individual in Dorset in 1969. This could represent a small overlooked resident population or a vagrant. There are further species of continental bats that could conceivably occur as vagrants.

The only species in immediate danger of extinction from Great Britain is the mouse-eared bat which is only known at one locality, but it may never have had more than a precarious foothold in Britain. The greater horseshoe bat, once widespread in the south-west, is declining in numbers and may need active conservation measures to save it, e.g. by protecting the caves used by roosting colonies from disturbance.

Finding mammals

The total of about thirty species mentioned earlier as potential inhabitants of any area in southern England can be broken down roughly as follows: hedgehog, mole, three shrews, six to ten bats, fox, stoat, weasel, mink, badger, otter, one to three deer, hare, rabbit, squirrel, five mice, rat and three voles. These need very different techniques for detection, so in this chapter I discuss in turn each line of enquiry that can be used in starting from scratch to survey an area. The next chapter will deal with each species or group of species in turn.

If you aim to detect the full diversity of species living in an area, you must diversify your methods of searching. The seven techniques discussed below can all contribute to a survey. Trapping of the smaller species, which might be considered the most obvious technique, is placed last since it is most demanding of equipment and time and is not always essential to a complete survey; though it can be productive, and gives the satisfaction of allowing you to handle the animals directly.

Asking questions

If the object of the exercise is to enjoy the detective work of tracking down each species unaided, you may wish to ignore this approach. But if speed and efficiency are important, then a lot can be learned by asking around, especially amongst people whose daily work may take them into contact with wild mammals, e.g. farmers, gamekeepers, foresters etc. With some species, like hedgehog, there is little possibility of getting erroneous information. But unless you are in a position to judge accurately your informant's competence in these matters, there are a number of pitfalls to look out for. Reports of hedgehog, as I have said, can normally be accepted at face value, as can those of fox and badger. At the opposite extreme, reports of bats may provide useful clues as to where to look yourself; but claims to have identified the species of bat in flight should be treated with extreme scepticism. In general it can be said that bats can only be critically identified 'in the hand' or when they can be examined at rest at very close range. Stoats and weasels are often confused, and that recent addition to our carnivorous fauna, the American mink, can cause difficulty by being mistaken for an otter or a polecat (or vice versa).

Foresters are usually very knowledgeable about the kinds of deer on their territory, but those who are less involved with deer may well be confused by the seasonal and individual variation shown by some species and care is required in accepting reports. Amongst the rodents, red and grey squirrel seem very distinct on the face of it, but it must be remembered that grey squirrels do show a certain amount of reddish brown at certain times and red squirrels become greyer in winter; both of these have led to cases of mistaken identity. A notorious source of confusion amongst rodents is provided by reports of 'water rats'. These can equally refer to water voles or to common rats, which are often very much at home in water. 'Harvest mouse' is another ambiguous term, being frequently used for any mice sent scurrying for safety by the harvester, including the ubiquitous wood mouse and house mouse just as often as the true harvest mouse. 'Field mouse' is also ambiguous, but in this case it is an ambiguous name rather than an ambiguous concept since it can refer equally to two very different creatures, the 'long-tailed field mouse', here called the wood mouse, and the 'short-tailed field mouse', here called the field vole.

But do not let all these problems of interpretation inhibit you from consulting those who know the countryside more intimately than you do. You will learn much and get many a clue that is worthy of your detective efforts.

Direct searching

Applying to mammals the normal technique of bird-watching – going into various suitable habitats and scrutinizing the country with the help of field glasses – will have limited, but useful, results. As with birds (but even more so), dawn and dusk are the most productive times of day. In this way, in appropriate habitats, one can reasonably expect to see squirrels, rabbits, hares, water vole, seals and deer; and especially at dawn one might hope for chance encounters with hedgehog or any of the carnivores, most of which are nocturnal.

Perhaps the most productive single approach in this category is to walk along the periphery of woodland at dawn. Squirrels will be active on the edge of the wood; rabbits will be feeding on open ground but within easy reach of cover and the same applies to the woodland deer, especially roe, fallow and sika. Hares are also very active at dawn. The best time to do any large scale surveying of hare distribution is probably in March. If brown hares are present, scrutiny of any field with short crops such as winter corn will probably reveal active hares around dawn and again in the hour before dusk. Water voles are perhaps most easily seen on straight drainage ditches, where a long stretch of water can be watched with field glasses. Again, a few minutes watching at such a site at dawn will usually reveal them if they are present.

For the small rodents and shrews, this kind of 'cold' watching is on the whole less productive; but one species that is especially worth looking for in this way is the bank vole. If a thicket of bramble, bracken or other low cover is kept under close observation for even ten minutes there is a reasonable chance that a bank vole will reveal itself, perhaps running along a fallen branch. Field voles and the shrews are equally diurnal, but tend to keep to denser cover like long grass and are less easily observed, while the mice are more distinctly nocturnal.

Direct observations of small rodents can sometimes be enhanced by regularly placing bait, e.g. seeds of any kind, at a particular spot and then keeping watch from nearby cover.

Another form of direct searching that can be very productive in finding small rodents and shrews, given the right circumstances, is by looking under logs, planks of wood and other such debris lying on the ground. Perhaps the ideal kind of 'cover' for this purpose consists of the sheets of corrugated iron that are (in other respects) all too frequently found strewn around the countryside. This operation is best carried out by two people, one to lift the cover quickly, the other to make a quick grab at any small mammal revealed, which can then be placed in a polythene bag or jar for observation. Common shrew seems to be the species most frequently found in this way but pygmy and water shrew are sometimes present, especially under planks of drift-wood on the storm-line of a beach. Amongst the rodents field vole is most often found. In the absence of a suitable container or net to clap over the animal, it is best caught by pinning it to the ground gently but firmly with the flat of one hand, grasping the scruff of the neck between finger and thumb of the other hand, then sliding the first hand back to grasp the *base* of the tail.

Searching for bats can take several forms. Watching at dusk will reveal feeding areas where bats are flying. These are most likely to be found on the edges of woods, in clearings, or over water. But some species do not emerge until it is fully dark and in any case none can be identified in flight with certainty without enormous experience. Watching potential roosting sites for bats emerging at dusk is useful. Buildings, bridges, hollow trees and caves are all worth watching. Searching potential roosting sites can be productive, especially after watching the bats emerging. Many roosts are virtually inaccessible, e.g. those of pipistrelles in wall cavities or under tiles, but roof-spaces, cellars, caves and tunnels may harbour bats. Horseshoe bats hang freely from the roof of a cave or cellar, but they are exceptional and most bats roost in crevices or flat against a vertical surface and can be very inconspicuous.

Remember that bats are very vulnerable to disturbance, especially in winter. Once found and identified they should be left strictly alone.

Looking for signs

Mammals of most species, large or small, leave signs of their presence which can provide useful clues in detecting the animals themselves and in some cases can allow precise identification of the species without ever seeing the maker of the sign. The most obvious signs are of course footprints, or spoor to use a technical name, but there are many others, such as nests, burrows, remains of food, droppings, scent and (in a slightly different category since it is part of the animal) hair. Although the study of signs can make fascinating detective work, in practical terms they should normally be treated as no more than a clue towards finding the animal itself. For the inexperienced there are very few signs that can by themselves provide really satisfactory evidence of a particular species. In the accounts of the different categories of sign below, prominence is given to those that can, with only a little experience, provide such evidence. Illustrations of many signs can be found in a field guide by Bang & Dahlstrom (see p.54).

Footprints The footprints of any one species vary enormously according to how the animal was moving and the nature of the ground. Major groups can be distinguished, e.g. deer (but confusion with sheep and goats is likely), squirrels, rabbit/hare, small rodents, shrews; but very few species can be precisely identified with any reasonable degree of certainty, and even in these cases more reliable kinds of evidence will normally be found without much difficulty.

There is not much point in making plaster casts of footprints with a view to submitting them to an expert, although experts can tell a great deal from an entire trail of prints *in situ*. However, in the case of a particularly puzzling trail that strongly suggests some species that is not otherwise known to be present in the area, a series of photographs might be worth taking.

Prints of otter can be distinctive (p. 14) and since river banks often provide good conditions for imprinting, and other methods of detection are difficult, they may constitute the best evidence that is easily available. Badger prints (p. 14) are equally distinctive but less often found and other evidence is usually available.

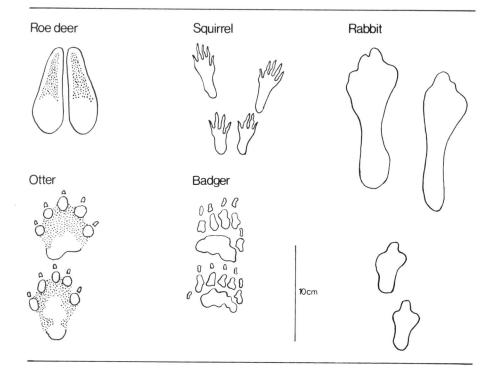

Roe deer   Squirrel   Rabbit

Otter   Badger

10cm

Prints of deer may be important in selecting vantage points for watching but are never conclusive by themselves. Likewise the beginner should not rely upon prints of fox, which are easily confused with dog, but nevertheless they may provide a guide towards better evidence.

Nests Nests of small rodents and shrews are most often found under logs etc. but they cannot be precisely identified in the absence of their owners. Likewise squirrel nests ('dreys') can with a little experience be distinguished from bird nests but do not by themselves allow identification of the species of squirrel.

The only nests that are worth searching for as a means of recording particular species are those of harvest mouse and, to a lesser extent, dormouse. In both cases only the summer nests, built above the ground, are easily found, but they are most easily found in winter when the vegetation is thinner (and the nests empty!). Harvest mouse nests are best searched for in winter in hedgerows and fences where long, spindly grass is supported by bushes or wire. The nests are very small spherical balls of closely woven grass, about 75 mm in diameter and without any obvious opening, attached to grass stems usually between 10 and 50 cm above the ground.

Nest of harvest mouse

Dormouse nests are less easily found by cold searching, but the place to look is in the branches of shrubs and small trees, especially where there is a dense tangle of creepers such as honeysuckle or clematis. Dormouse nests are never made entirely of grass and they usually have an opening. But without experience empty nests cannot safely be distinguished from birds' nests. Dormice will however make use of old birds' nests and even nest boxes and these are worth examining.

Burrows The species responsible for a burrow or other evidence of tunnelling can usually be determined, although this is often facilitated by associated signs such as droppings, scent or hair. Large burrows, say over 20 cm in diameter, are usually the work of either a fox or a badger.

A badger 'set' usually has a number of openings sometimes separated by several metres. Each has a large heap of earth in front of the hole, and close inspection can usually reveal characteristic hairs amongst the spoil or caught on thorns or twigs near the opening. The long, rather stiff black and white hairs are distinctive. Foxes may occupy old badger holes, but otherwise their burrows usually have no more than two openings and are smaller and shallower than those of a badger, with much less of a spoil heap. Again hairs that are found may be distinctive. A piece of sticky tape stretched across the top of a hole overnight will, if properly placed, pick up hairs of any animal entering or leaving.

Badger set

Otters tend to live in enlarged natural crevices, under a tree or amongst rocks, rather than in specially excavated burrows. These dens, or 'holts', can best be identified by the smooth pathways leading from them and the presence of food remains such as fish bones or, near the sea, crab shells.

Rabbit burrows, if they are occupied, can always be identified as such by droppings (see below).

Holes of small rodents and shrews cannot provide firm evidence of the species concerned, but rat-sized holes in river banks are worth watching to see water vole or common rat.

The mole is one species that can be quite satisfactorily identified by its excavations. Mole hills occur in groups; they are symmetrical and without an opening, and they are usually flattened long before they become covered with vegetation. Similar heaps that remain steep-sided and bear a crop of plants (often topped by rabbit droppings) are likely to be hills of the yellow ant. From a distance cowpats can also be mistaken for mole-hills. Under some special circumstances, e.g. on some small islands, water voles may produce heaps resembling mole-hills but these are not symmetrical and have an opening at one side.

Remains of food A deliberate search for signs of an animal's feeding activity is not normally a profitable way to detect species nor to identify them precisely. But chance finds may provide some useful clues. Amongst carnivores, the remains of the prey of fox and otter may be distinctive. When a fox kills a bird such as a pigeon, it removes the wing feathers by biting them off rather than by pulling them out. However, this should not by itself be considered conclusive evidence of fox. Otters will often leave pieces of fish or crabs which again the inexperienced should treat as suggestive rather than conclusive.

All rodents will eat acorns and other nuts, but not all species will hoard them. On the basis of a single, gnawed nut, squirrels, which make large openings with coarse edges, can be distinguished from mice, which make small openings with narrow tooth marks. Hoards of nuts or grain found (for example) under a log are the property of wood mouse, yellow-necked mouse or harvest mouse, not of voles, house mouse or rats, none of which normally store food.

Droppings Droppings can provide sufficient evidence to identify a small number of species. Probably the ones most worth searching for are those of otter, known as 'spraints'. Spraints serve for communication amongst otters and are deposited at particular prominent sites such as large boulders in a stream or on a grassy tussock. They are black when fresh but rapidly bleach. They have a characteristic smell and consist largely of fish bones, crab shells etc.

Two species of rodents can usefully be identified by their droppings. If runways in grass are searched, piles of olive green droppings, about 5 mm long with rounded ends, may be found, covered with cut lengths of fresh grass. These are a sure sign of field vole. Concentrations of similar but larger (c. 8 mm) droppings near water indicate water vole.

The droppings of hedgehog, often found on meadows or on lawns, are usually distinctive: they are cylindrical, with pointed ends, 2–3 cm in length and usually black and composed largely of insect fragments.

Droppings of deer can provide valuable evidence of their behaviour and movements but by themselves do not help much in identifying the species concerned. Roosting places of bats can sometimes be located by the accumulation of droppings on the ground below. These are small, irregular and composed entirely of insect cuticle. They can be found in hollow trees, fireplaces of empty houses, church porches etc.

Scent Probably the only species that can usefully and conclusively be identified by scent alone, at least by the relatively inexperienced person, is the fox. The characteristic scent is in the urine, and both sexes use urination to mark territory.

Hair The use of shed hairs to confirm the use of a hole by badger or fox has already been mentioned. Hairs of these species can also be found where trails pass under barbed fences or thorny bushes. But unless there is enough of the characteristic black and white guard hair to identify badger there is little point in attempting precise identification. Although most species can be identified by careful examination of hair it is time-consuming and the species concerned can usually be more economically identified in other ways.

Road casualties

All the species of mammals dealt with here, apart from the seals, are liable to be killed by traffic on the roads, but some are particularly vulnerable, to the extent that a deliberate search of roads is a very quick and efficient way of recording certain species. For several reasons, not least to avoid becoming a road casualty oneself, such a search is best done on secondary roads in early morning and a bicycle is probably the most suitable means of transport. Hedgehog, common rat, stoat, weasel, rabbit and hare are the species most often found, but voles and shrews are also frequently killed although more easily overlooked. Some very significant records of rare bats have been obtained in this way since there is no bias against those species whose roosting sites are difficult to locate.

Some species, such as hedgehog or badger, present no problems of identification even if badly squashed. Stoat and weasel can usually be identified easily by the tail; rabbit and hare by the ears (which can be collected for closer examination if there is any doubt).

If small rodents and shrews cannot be identified precisely on the spot they can be taken home in a polythene bag or it may be practicable to extract the skull or lower jaw which can later be identified by the teeth (but this is difficult in the case of the wood mouse and yellow-necked mouse). In the case of bats it is always worth preserving as much as possible until you are quite certain of the identification.

Dead animals, in various stages of decomposition, may of course be found in places other than on roads. It is helpful to appreciate that all British mammals can be identified by a skull alone, even if badly damaged, and many by a single lower jaw, or even a single tooth. The tables and keys in the next chapter enable entire skulls to be identified. Fragments or separate teeth can best be identified by comparison with a reference collection of entire skulls.

Bottles

If discarded bottles are lying in an appropriate position they often entrap small rodents or shrews which squeeze in, perhaps attracted by the odour of the former contents or by insects, and cannot get out again. Such bottles are all too common in hedgerows, roadside grass, in bushes around picnic sites and in rubbish dumps. For those with a strong stomach they may provide a very quick and effective way of determining which species of small mammals are present. The bottle may contain a revolting soup from which skulls or lower jaws can be isolated and either identified on the spot by examining the teeth with a hand lens, or carried home in tightly stoppered containers. The sites of grass or shrub fires are especially worth examining and may have the advantage of a dry catch.

With a little practice all species can be identified in the field from the skulls and teeth, except that wood mouse and yellow-necked cannot be separated. If skulls of these are preserved they can usually be identified by very careful measurement (p. 27) but it is usually better to rely upon other ways of detecting these species.

Orthodox glass milk bottles are by far the most productive of small mammals, while common shrew and bank vole are the species most frequently found. However, water shrews seem to be found in numbers that are disproportional to those revealed by trapping and often in what appear to be very unpromising habitats.

18

Bird pellets

Both the owls and the diurnal birds of prey regurgitate pellets that contain the bones and fur of their mammalian prey, along with feathers, insect cuticle etc. from other prey. Concentrations of pellets can sometimes be found under favourite resting sites, for example under a barn owl's nest in a farm building, in the fireplace of an empty house or under an isolated tree or post in open country.

Owl pellet and contents

Pellets are not objectionable to handle and are best pulled apart gently when they are slightly moist. Although much of interest can be learned from a detailed study of the contents of a pellet, for basic identification of the species of prey it is sufficient to isolate the skulls with or without the lower jaws and usually without the braincase which easily breaks off (barn owls in particular produce relatively undamaged skulls). With a little practice such skulls are easily identified, although again it is difficult to distinguish between wood mice and yellow-necked mice.

Pellets do not tell you where the prey was living and the possibility of its having been caught some distance away must be considered. However owls, which on the whole produce the most useful pellets, are mainly rather sedentary birds with limited feeding ranges.

Trapping

As a technique of locating and identifying mammals, trapping is most relevant in the case of the mouse-sized rodents and shrews. The traps used may be designed to kill or to catch alive. The latter is obviously the more satisfactory from many points of view, but killing traps also have their advantages. A more detailed guide to trapping for the purpose of collecting and preserving mammals is given in a separate booklet published by the British Museum (Natural History) (see p. 54).

Break-back mouse traps These have the advantage of being cheap, readily available, easily portable in quantities and easily hidden when set. Many makes are not sensitive enough to catch pygmy shrews. When they are set overnight in a good habitat, e.g. a hedgerow, one can expect a success rate of between 10 and 30 per cent. As few as ten traps can therefore produce useful results, but in order to have a high chance of catching the scarcer species several hundred

Pitfall trap

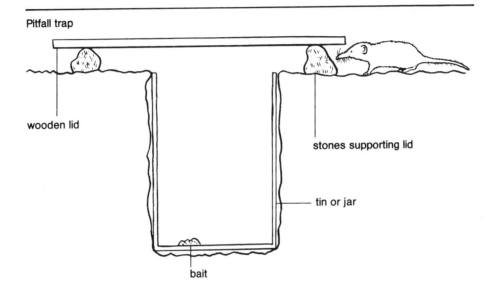

wooden lid

stones supporting lid

tin or jar

bait

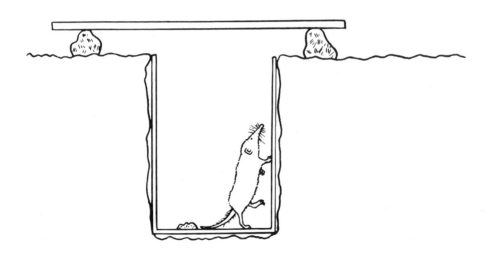

Seesaw trap

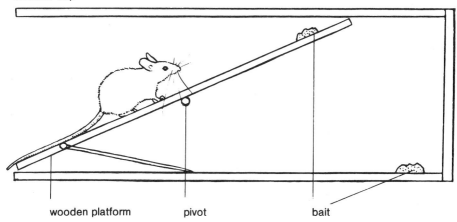

wooden platform   pivot   bait

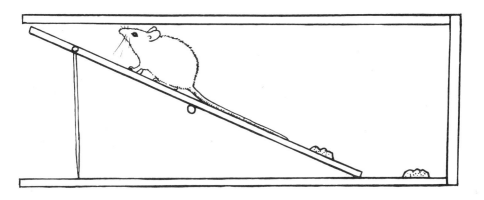

trap-nights may be required. A good general-purpose bait is peanut butter mixed with oats or other cereal, but some kinds of traps are quite effective without bait if they are set in runways such as are easily found in many habitats, e.g. on woodland banks and in long grass. The most important single factor to consider in choosing a site is cover, whether it is shrub, long grass or rocks.

In most circumstances one need have no fears about seriously reducing the population by break-back trapping. Any loss will be small by comparison with natural predation and all the common small mammals have an enormous capacity to make good any loss. The scarcer species, such as the dormouse, are so difficult to trap that again there is little chance of depleting the population.

Live traps The only live trap for small rodents and shrews readily available commercially in Britain is the Longworth, made by the Longworth Scientific Instrument Co., Abingdon, Berks. But many different kinds can be devised at home and some ideas to copy may be found in a book by Bateman (p. 54). Live traps should be provided with dry grass and food (any grain for rodents) and should be protected from the sun as well as from potential disturbance. Shrews do not survive well in traps and are likely to be found dead unless the traps can be examined every three or four hours.

To examine one's catch it is best to open the trap in a large polythene bag. The animal can then be examined in the bag before being released. As with break-back traps, one can expect to catch all three species of shrew and all the small species of rodent except for harvest mouse and dormouse which will only rarely be caught even where they are most abundant. The possibility of catching a weasel adds to the wisdom of opening a trap cautiously.

Pitfalls A pitfall is basically a hole in the ground into which you hope an animal will fall. To increase the chances of this happening various elaborations can be contrived. The first is to provide unscalable walls by sinking a rigid container − a jar or tin − or by lining the hole with a cylinder of flexible plastic. The hole should be covered with a piece of wood propped up on stones a couple of centimetres above the rim. This keeps out the rain and also provides an attractive crevice to entice animals into the pit. A hole about 30 cm deep is adequate for shrews and voles but mice may require something rather deeper to contain them. Pitfalls should be provided with food and should not be left open and unattended for more than a day. But since they can be left *in situ* but closed, they are useful for periodic monitoring of the small mammal fauna of a locality (see p. 20.)

Identifying mammals

There are many books available with coloured illustrations of British mammals (see p. 54). In practice however, as detailed in the last chapter, only a minority of identifications will involve direct sightings of living, free animals and the purpose of this chapter is to consider the problems of critical identification that actually arise in dealing with each group of mammals and each kind of evidence. Throughout, the emphasis is on surveying the present mammalian fauna. Some of the identification procedures may also be useful in the study of subfossil bones, e.g. from archaeological sites. Almost any bone or tooth can be identified if studied in sufficient detail, but whereas an isolated humerus may be the only available evidence of a species in a fossil stratum, the attempted identification of a humerus picked up on the surface of the ground would rarely be the most effective way of recording the present existence of any species in the neighbourhood. Most such isolated finds can be efficiently identified, if this is considered worth the effort, only by direct comparison with a reference collection, although there are some published illustrations that are helpful (see p. 54 – Lawrence & Brown).

The guide to identification that follows is divided into eight sections. An animal can easily be allocated to the appropriate section by its superficial appearance as follows.

Shrews, mice and small voles

This group comprises all small mammals, other than bats, having the head and body less than 130 mm, i.e. those likely to be caught in Longworth or similar live-traps, or in mouse-sized breakbacks, or found as remains in owl pellets or bottles. The young of larger species such as water voles or rats can usually be recognized by their disproportionately large hind feet (over 25 mm even in half-grown animals) and, in the case of skulls, by unworn or unerupted teeth and general fragility.

With experience many species can be identified on the basis of brief glimpses 'in the wild' but this is easier if you first become familiar with them 'in the hand'.

Shrews can be distinguished from rodents by their pointed muzzle and continuous rows of teeth.

Common shrew

All species of shrews can readily be found under logs and planks, in bottles, in owl pellets or by trapping. They are about fully grown by the time they leave the nest and there are no milk teeth to confuse identification.

The three species present on the mainland of Britain all have red-tipped teeth and can be distinguished as follows.

	Pygmy shrew	Common shrew	Water shrew
Colour of back	Brown	Brown	Black
Keel of stiff white hairs under tail	No	No	Yes
Fringes of stiff white hairs on feet	Slight	Slight	Prominent
Length of head and body	40–60 mm	60–80 mm	70–90 mm
Length of hind feet, without claws	10–11 mm	12–13 mm	17–18 mm
Tail: head and body	65–70%	50–60%	60–75%
Length of upper tooth-row	6.2–6.6 mm	8.0–8.8 mm	9.6–10.2 mm
Teeth (unworn)			

On the Channel and Scilly Islands white-toothed shrews occur, distinguished by: absence of red on teeth; scattered long bristles on tail; greyer pelage; only three upper unicuspid teeth. The two species are difficult to distinguish but so far have not been found on the same island.

	White-toothed shrews	
	Lesser	Greater
Length of head and body	50–75 mm	60–90 mm
Length of hind feet	10–13 mm	10.5–14 mm
Length of upper tooth-row	7.4–8.0 mm	7.7–8.5 mm
Teeth (unworn)		

Mice and voles are rodents, with a shorter and wider muzzle than shrews and with chisel-shaped incisor teeth (always yellow or orange), separated by a long gap from the chewing molar teeth.

The dormouse is unmistakable by its bushy tail, bright orange-brown colour and, in the skull, by having *four* cheek-teeth in each row, with a unique pattern of transverse ridges.

Dormouse

They spend most of their time in bushy growth off the ground. They are difficult to trap and are rarely found in owl pellets. They are best located by searching for nests and by looking in bird nesting boxes.

The very local fat dormouse is grey and is much larger – see p. 30.

Mice have long tails (about equal in length to head and body combined), and have a complex pattern of rounded tubercles on the cheek-teeth (which are rooted).

Wood mouse

Harvest mice may be difficult to trap and are most readily located by searching for the small round nests woven into grass stems in hedgerows etc. (p. 15). The other species are easily trapped and usually occur abundantly in owl pellets. The four species of mice are distinguished as follows:

	Harvest	House
Colour of back	Yellowish brown	Greyish brown
Colour of underside	Very pale grey	Greyish brown
Yellow mark on chest	None	None
Length of head and body	50–70 mm	70–90 mm
Length of hind feet	13–15 mm	17–19 mm
Length of ear	7–9 mm	12–15 mm
Length of upper cheek-teeth	2.6–2.8 mm	2.9–3.4 mm
No. of roots on 1st upper cheek-tooth	5	3
Profile of upper incisors		

	Wood	Yellow-necked
Colour of back	Reddish brown	Reddish brown
Colour of underside	Grey	Pale grey
Yellow mark on chest	Small streak	Broad collar
Length of head and body	80–100 mm	90–120 mm
Length of hind feet	20–23 mm	23–25 mm
Length of ear	15–17 mm	16–18 mm
Length of upper cheek-teeth	3.6–4.2 mm	4.0–4.4 mm
No. of roots on 1st upper cheek-tooth	4	4
Profile of upper incisors	As harvest mouse	As harvest mouse

Isolated skulls of wood mouse and yellow-necked mouse cannot always be distinguished with certainty. If precise measurement is possible, using a microscope, the anterior-posterior thickness of the upper incisors is useful:

1.10 – 1.30 mm: wood mouse;

1.45 – 1.65 mm: yellow-necked mouse.

Specimens falling between these values should be considered unidentifiable unless the cheek-teeth are very worn, in which case it will be an old wood mouse, or completely unworn in which case it will be a young yellow-necked mouse.

The small voles have short tails (not more than half the length of head and body), short ears, and flat-crowned cheek-teeth with a complex pattern of enamel ridges.

Field vole

Voles are easily trapped, occur abundantly in owl pellets and in bottles, and can often be found under logs and planks. The field vole (and the Orkney/Guernsey vole) makes characteristic runways in grass, identifiable by the presence of piles of olive green droppings covered by chopped leaves of fresh grass.
The three species are distinguished as follows:

	Bank vole	Field vole	Orkney/ Guernsey vole
Colour of back	Reddish brown	Yellowish or greyish brown	
Tail: head and body	c. 50%	c. 30%	c. 30%
Left 2nd upper cheek-teeth			

The Orkney/Guernsey vole is confined to these islands (and the continent) and has not been found together with the common field vole anywhere in Britain.

Mole and hedgehog

The mole can be recorded quite satisfactorily by the presence of mole-hills (see p. 16). If the animal itself is found, alive or dead, it cannot easily be mistaken for anything else.

Mole

The skull is occasionally found in owl pellets – note the carnivore-like canines combined with the slender muzzle of the insectivore (compare for example the weasel, p. 38). A very characteristic bone of the mole is the humerus which is as wide as it is long – an adaptation to a burrowing mode of life.

The hedgehog likewise cannot be mistaken for anything else, even for the much larger, black and white porcupines that have sometimes escaped from zoos. Hedgehogs can be found by searching lawns and meadows with a torch at night; and by looking for road casualties.

Hedgehog

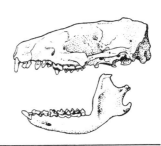

The skull is robust for an insectivore and lacks prominent canines.

Large rodents

Large rodents comprise seven species that are rarely caught in mouse-sized traps and rarely found in owl pellets. They can be seen 'in the wild' more readily than the smaller species and most of them can best be recorded by direct observation.

Squirrels are easily seen. Grey squirrels could conceivably be confused with fat dormice but the latter are very local, strictly nocturnal and very much smaller (see below). Red and grey squirrel are easily distinguished provided it is realized that grey squirrels can have a considerable tinge of brown on the back. Red squirrels are a rich deep reddish brown above and have prominent tufts on their ears in winter.

Red squirrel

The fat dormouse is like a half-sized grey squirrel with an even bushier tail. In the hand the short slender hind feet (25–35mm) distinguish it from a half-grown grey squirrel. It is nocturnal and difficult to detect unless it can be trapped when it enters attics and farm buildings in autumn, especially in upper floors where fruit is stored. It is also worth looking for it in cavities in trees and in bird nest boxes.

Fat dormouse

Rats and water voles can be trapped in rat-sized traps but are not difficult to observe. However, records of ship rats are best confirmed by trapping. Common rats are usually frequent amongst road casualties. Avoid assuming that a swimming 'rat' must be a water vole – common rats may be almost as aquatic as water voles.

The three species can be distinguished as follows:

	Water vole	Common rat	Ship rat
Fur	Soft and shaggy	Stiff and sleek	Stiff and sleek
Tail: head and body	55–70%	70–90%	100–130%
Length of hind foot	27–37mm	40–45mm	30–40mm
Length of ear	16–18mm	19–22mm	24–27mm
Muzzle	Blunt	Rather pointed	More pointed
Cheek-teeth	Similar to field vole	Similar to wood mouse	Similar to wood mouse
Skull shape			

Common rat

Water vole

Colour can be confusing. Water voles are usually brown but may be black, especially in northern Scotland. Common rats are usually brown, but ship rats – 'black rats' – may be anything from brown to black.

The coypu is a very large aquatic rodent now confined to East Anglia. It is very much larger than water vole and common rat – adults up to 600mm in length of head and body. Compared with an otter it is much shorter and fatter and the tail is thin. Young animals comparable in size to a water vole or common rat are unlikely to be on their own.

The skull is easily distinguished by its large size and by the *four* vole-like cheek-teeth in each row. The tooth-rows are close together in front and diverge widely behind.

Rabbit, hares and wallaby

Hares and rabbits cannot easily be mistaken for anything else but the three species can be rather difficult to distinguish from each other.

	Rabbit	Brown hare	Mountain hare
Top of tail	Black	Black	White
Ears	All brown	Black tips	Black tips
Length of ears from notch	60-70mm	85–105mm	60–80mm
Length of hind feet	75–95mm	115–150mm	120–155mm
Palate		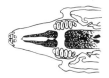	
Curvature of upper incisors			

Brown hare   Mountain hare   Rabbit

In Britain the mountain hare turns more or less completely white in winter, but the ear-tips always remain black. The Irish race of the same species remains brown throughout the year.

Wallabies are comparable to hares in size and sitting posture but differ in their short ears, long thick tail and, at least when travelling fast, their hopping gait without using the front feet.

The skull of a wallaby is very distinctive, with three pairs of incisors above, arranged in a V, and a single pair below pointing directly forwards as in shrews. There is a long gap between the incisors and the cheek-teeth which number five or six in each row.

All these species can be observed directly but in addition rabbits and hares are frequent as road casualties. Rabbits can also be satisfactorily identified on the basis of the association of burrows and droppings, the latter being spherical, about 7–8mm in diameter and deposited at regular sites, frequently on mounds such as ant-hills. Droppings of hares are larger (12–13mm), slightly flattened, usually dispersed and more easily confused with those of small deer.

Wallaby

Carnivores

The ten species of carnivores in the British Isles are predominantly nocturnal animals, and some can be very difficult to detect. They are all fairly distinctive if seen well, but too often only a brief glimpse in poor light is all that we get. They can be considered in three groups based on size.

Small (head and body less than 300mm)	Weasel and stoat
Medium (head and body 300–500mm)	Marten, polecat, ferret and mink
Large (head and body over 500mm)	Fox, badger, otter and wild cat

Weasel and stoat are very substantially smaller than any of the others – a large stoat reaches 280mm (head and body) – and the sharp contrast between white under parts and reddish-brown back and sides is not found in any of the larger members of the weasel family. Both are moderately diurnal and are most often seen dashing across a road or peering out from cover such as a dry-stone wall or wood-pile. They can be caught in mouse- or rat-sized live traps. Although there is a considerable difference in size, the black terminal part of the stoat's tail (persisting even in white winter coat) is the only really safe character when an animal is seen 'in the field'.

Weasel   Stoat

Skulls can be clearly distinguished from those of other carnivores by their small size (see table overleaf), but it is not always possible to separate stoat and weasel skulls with certainty.

Marten, polecat, ferret and mink all have long sinuous bodies but are much larger and heavier than stoats. They are more strictly nocturnal and are consequently difficult to observe. But they are also difficult to trap, and their dens are less conspicuous than, for example, those of foxes and badgers; therefore direct sightings, along with road causalties, remain the chief means of detection.

Martens are the only ones that are likely to be seen in trees (but they also spend much of their time on the ground). The large pale area on the throat is diagnostic, but smaller and usually more irregular pale patches are found on the throat in some forms of mink.

Polecat and mink are very easily confused and it is usually necessary to see the characteristic facial pattern of polecat to be certain. Feral ferrets range in colour from pure albinos to dark animals scarcely distinguishable from wild polecats, but usually the overall colour is pale and in particular the white on the face is more extensive.

Polecat   Mink

Marten

Individual records of ferrets or polecat-ferrets are worth noting, but it is very desirable to follow up such reports to try to establish whether the animal has itself escaped from captivity or is a member of a population that is well established and breeding in the wild. In the case of a dead polecat-ferret of doubtful status the skull should be examined. The postorbital region is usually narrower in ferrets than in polecats: under 16mm in ferret, over 16mm in polecat.

Mink are usually found near water and are substantially smaller than otters. The tail in particular is much thinner and shorter than that of an otter. Most wild mink are a uniform dark brown with only a little white under the mouth; but many colour varieties are bred for fur and these are sometimes found in wild populations.

Fox, badger, otter and cat are all very distinctive if they are seen at all well. The fox is unique in being easily identified by its scent. Both fox and badger holes are rather distinctive, and badger sets in particular can usually be safely identified as such without seeing the occupants (see p.16). Otters can often be seen by watching suitable waterside habitats in the early morning; however, their presence can also be satisfactorily confirmed by their droppings (p. 17) or by the characteristic food remains outside a holt. When considering otter, however, the possibility of mink must always be kept in mind.

Otter

The wild cat cannot easily be confused with any other wild species but the problem of confusion with more or less feral domestic cats is a difficult one. Brief glimpses of cats at dusk or in the headlights of a car can rarely result in a satisfactory identification. When seen well, or when a corpse is available, the wild cat can be identified by the shorter, bushier tail and generally large size. But any record of an individual away from the normal range is worth investigating to establish if a population of uniformly 'wild-type' animals is present.

Wild cat

Skulls of carnivores are sometimes found, e.g. in the spoil heap outside a burrow. The following table and figures should allow the identification of most skulls. All have rather prominent, conical canines above and below, continuous tooth-rows, and considerable diversity of shape and size amongst the post-canine teeth of any single skull. The measurements in the Table apply only to adult skulls with all teeth fully erupted. The post-orbital constriction is the narrow waist on the upper surface of the skull nearest to the brain-case (see figure).

Species	Overall length	Upper canine to last molar incl.	No. of post-canine teeth Upper	Lower	Width of post-orbital constriction
Weasel	32–42mm	8–11mm	4	5	7–9mm
Stoat	42–53mm	10–15mm	4	5	9–12mm
Mink	60–72mm	19–22mm	4	5	10–13mm
Polecat	58–71mm	16–20mm	4	5	16–18mm
Ferret	53-71mm	16–20mm	4	5	12–16mm
Marten	77–90mm	27–33mm	5	6	16–22mm
Cat	85–100mm	27–32mm	4	3	27–35mm
Otter	105–125mm	31–38mm	5	5	12–15mm
Badger	116–135mm	38–45mm	4 or 5	5 or 6	24–26mm
Fox	135–160mm	60–70mm	6	7	21–24mm

Skulls of dogs vary enormously according to the breed but most have the jaws shorter and the teeth more crowded than in the fox.

Dog (Irish wolf-hound)

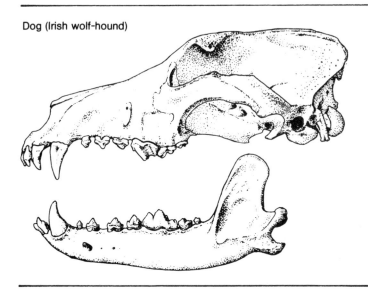

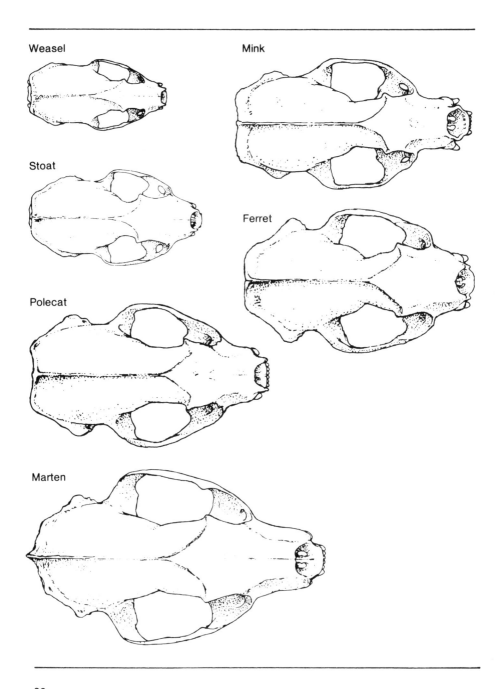

Weasel

Mink

Stoat

Ferret

Polecat

Marten

38

Cat

Otter

Badger

Fox

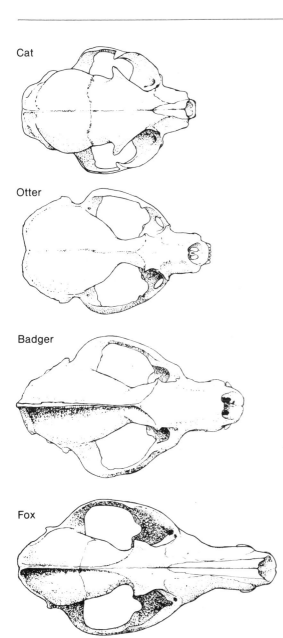

Seals

Only two species of seal, the common and the grey, occur regularly on British coasts, but for the inexperienced they can be very difficult to distinguish with certainty. Most often only a head is seen above the water. Both species may be found hauled out ashore, especially on rocky islets or sand banks. On rocks they can be remarkably inconspicuous in spite of their size, and careful scrutiny of suitable rocks with binoculars will often reveal animals that would otherwise be overlooked.

Although there are differences in size and in the pattern of spots, the only really conclusive characters in practice are in the head as tabulated below. Female and young male grey seals have the forehead less convex but never conspicuously concave as in common seals.

	Common seal	Grey seal
Maximum length	2m	2.5m
Spots	Small and numerous	Larger and fewer
Forehead in profile	Concave	Straight or convex
Nostrils (seen from front)	Meet at bottom to form V ('V for *vitulina*')	Widely separated

Common seal Grey seal

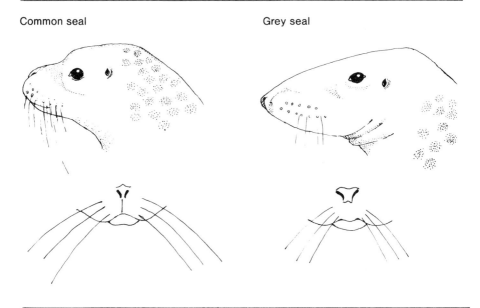

Skulls of seals are large (160–300mm if adult), and have continuous tooth-rows and prominent canines as in carnivores. The post-canine teeth are rather uniform in shape, being narrow with one prominent and two or three smaller cusps.

Four species of Arctic seals, and the walrus, are very rare vagrants in British waters, especially around Shetland. Adults are reasonably distinctive, but juveniles, which are often the ones that wander to the south, are more difficult to distinguish from our local seals.

Ringed seal: like common seal but spots larger and surrounded by pale rings.

Harp seal: white with black head and irregular black patch on back.

Bearded seal: uniform brown, whiskers very prominent.

Hooded seal: like grey seal but blotches larger and more irregular. Adult male can inflate his muzzle but is unlikely to do so away from the breeding ground; therefore not likely to be distinguishable from grey seal without considerable experience.

Walrus: juveniles lack tusks, but uniform colour, very broad bristly muzzle and thick neck distinctive. Hind feet point forwards on land.

Common seals

Bats

With experience it is possible to identify bats found at a roost without handling them. To acquire this skill however it is necessary to handle them; but handling should be kept to an absolute minimum, and hibernating bats in particular should not be disturbed repeatedly. Without long experience bats cannot be identified precisely in flight. The following guide therefore presumes access to a bat, alive or dead, in the hand.

Measurement of the forearm (see figure) is very useful in identification. However, it is important to be able to recognize young animals in which the wing bones are not fully grown. If the extended wing is examined against a bright light, pale spots on either side of each joint indicate unossified cartilage and therefore subadult size.

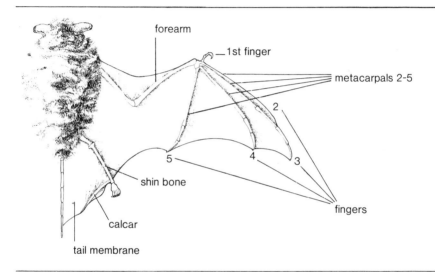

British bats fall into two very clear-cut groups, as follows.

Horseshoe bats have a very conspicuous and complex system of fleshy lobes around the nostrils. The two species are easily distinguished by size:

Greater horseshoe – forearm 52–56mm
Lesser horseshoe – forearm 35–40mm

(Three additional species of horseshoe bat occur in continental Europe but have not so far been recorded in Britain. All have forearms intermediate in length between those of the greater and lesser horseshoes and differ in the detailed structure of the nose-leaf.)

Vespertilionid bats have no nose-leaves, but have a fleshy lobe, the tragus, arising from the lower margin of the ear opening just in front of the notch. The size and shape of the tragus is a useful guide to identification. The following key uses only external characters easily visible in a live bat provided that a millimetre rule is available. Identification of skulls is dealt with on p. 46.

Greater horseshoe bat and detail of noseleaf

To use the key start with paragraph 1 and decide which of the alternatives applies. The first alternative (ears joined) leads to paragraph 2; if the second alternative applies (ears separated) go straight to paragraph 4. Proceed in this way until the name of a bat is reached.

1	Bases of ears joined together on crown of head ..	See 2
	Bases of ears widely separated	See 4
2	Ears very long (32–40mm)	See 3
	Ears short (13–16mm); forearm 36–39mm; very dark brown, with silky fur	Barbastelle
3	Fur of back usually yellowish brown, basal parts of hairs brown (blow fur to make a parting); greatest width of tragus 4.5–5.5mm; (forearm 35–41mm)	Common long-eared bat
	Fur of back grey or greyish brown, basal parts of hairs slaty grey; greatest width of tragus 5.6–6.2mm; (forearm 38–43mm)	Grey long-eared bat
	(In the case of dead animals always confirm identification of long-eared bats by the skull.)	
4	Tragus slender and pointed (species of *Myotis*) ..	See 5
	Tragus short and rounded or truncate	See 10
5	Forearm 58–71mm	Mouse-eared bat
	Forearm under 50mm	See 6
	(The lesser mouse-eared bat, which may occur in Britain, has a forearm of 53–63mm and is not clearly separable from the mouse-eared bat by external characters.) ..	

6	Margin of tail membrane densely fringed with short hairs, especially between the end of the calcar and the tail; tragus distinctly more than half length of ear; (greyish brown above, white below, forearm 36–40mm) ..	Natterer's bat
	Tail membrane hairless, or hairs few and scattered; tragus about half length of ear or shorter	See 7
7	Ears very long, extending more than 6mm beyond tip of nose when laid forwards; forearm 40–43mm; (greyish brown above, white below)	Bechstein's bat
	Ears short, extending no more than 4mm beyond nose; forearm 31–38mm	See 8
8	Feet large, distinctly more than half length of shin; calcar long, extending about two-thirds way from heel to tail; first joint of middle (third) finger longer than second; face pale; (forearm 37–38mm)	Water bat
	Feet small, not more than half length of shin; calcar short, extending about half way to tail; first and second joints of middle finger equal	See 9
9	Upper side very dark brown; penis uniformly thin; .. (forearm 31–36mm)	Whiskered bat
	Upper side yellowish brown; penis club-shaped; (forearm 33–38mm)	Brandt's bat
	(Where practicable identification of these should be confirmed by critical examination of the skull.)	
10	Forearm over 46mm	See 11
	Forearm under 46mm	See 12
11	Tail projecting about 6mm beyond membrane; metacarpals of fourth and fifth fingers equal; (forearm 49–53mm) ..	Serotine
	Tail not projecting beyond membrane; metacarpal of fourth finger as long as metacarpal and first phalanx of fifth (i.e. wings long and narrow); (fur bright golden brown; forearm 47–55mm)	Noctule
12	Forearm over 38mm	See 13
	Forearm under 38mm	See 14
13	Upper surface uniform dark brown, underside only slightly lighter; (forearm 39–43mm)	Leisler's bat
	Upper surface brown with white tips of hairs giving a frosted effect, underside almost white; (forearm 43–45mm)	Parti-coloured bat
14	Forearm 27–32mm; wings narrow, fifth finger (from wrist) about 40mm; thumbs short, length about equal to width of wrist	Pipistrelle
	Forearm 32–35mm; wings wider, fifth finger about 46mm; thumbs long, length much greater than width of wrist ..	Nathusius' pipistrelle

Ear of Serotine bat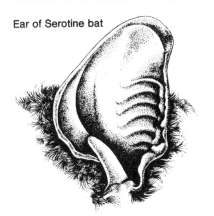

Noctule bat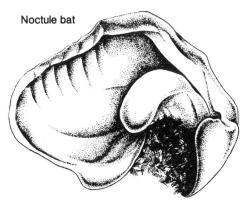

Natterer's bat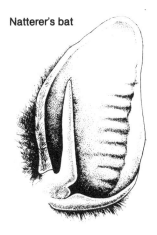

Tail membrane and foot of Water bat

Natterer's bat

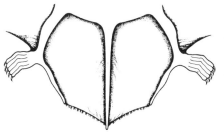 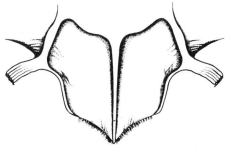

Bat skulls can sometimes be found on the floors of caves and other roost-sites, and very rarely in owl pellets. They can be recognized as such by the continuous tooth-rows, enlarged canines and small size (under 25mm).

Skulls of horseshoe bats have two bulbous projections on the upper surface just behind the nasal cavity, and the upper incisors are borne on a slender median premaxillary bone that is easily detached. The two species are very different in size.

Total length over 18mm; upper tooth-row 8.2–8.8mm – Greater horseshoe.

Total length under 18mm; upper tooth-row 5.2–5.6mm – Lesser horseshoe.

Skulls of vespertilionid bats lack bulbous projections and have the upper incisors widely separated on either side of a median cavity. They can mostly be identified by the combination of number of teeth and length of upper tooth-row, as in the following table. However, this does not enable all species to be distinguished, and all such identifications should be confirmed by comparison with a reference collection or more detailed descriptions.

| Species | No. of post-canine teeth on each side | | Upper canine to last molar |
	Upper	Lower	
Mouse-eared	6	6	9.8–10.4mm
Lesser mouse-eared	6	6	8.0–9.4mm
Bechstein's	6	6	6.8–7.0mm
Natterer's	6	6	5.6–6.2mm
Water	6	6	5.0–5.2mm
Whiskered	6	6	4.8–5.4mm
Brandt's	6	6	5.2–5.6mm
Common long-eared	5	6	4.8–5.5mm
Grey long-eared	5	6	5.8–6.2mm
Noctule	5	5	6.8–7.4mm
Leisler's	5	5	5.8–6.0mm
Barbastelle	5	5	4.6–4.8mm
Pipistrelle	5	5	4.0–4.2mm
Nathusius' pipistrelle	5	5	4.4–5.0mm
Serotine	4	5	7.6–8.2mm
Parti-coloured	4	5	5.0–5.4mm

Lesser horseshoe bat

Common long-eared bat

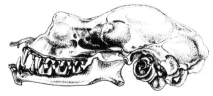

Deer and other ungulates

The presence of deer can usually be detected by looking for tracks and droppings, but to identify the species concerned it is necessary to get a good view of the animals themselves. This is best done by watching suitable feeding places, such as clearings in woodland, at dawn or dusk. Chance encounters, especially in woodland, usually result in a fleeting view of the hind quarters – which fortunately are rather distinctive. Wild goats are virtually confined to open hills and rocky coasts.

Sometimes shed antlers are found. These are usually diagnostic if they are well developed, but antlers of young bucks may not be clearly identifiable.

In the following descriptions unique characters are italicized. Remember that male deer are without antlers at certain seasons (usually in spring). All females lack antlers but have the same rump and tail patterns as the males.

Red deer: *large size;* unspotted (except calf); yellowish white rump with short brown tail; male with mane on neck; *antlers with three points* (tines) projecting forward from lower half of beam (but young animals may have only two as in sika).

Fallow: spotted coat (or may be uniform and very dark); white rump bounded by black, *tail long and with central dark stripe; antlers usually flattened at tip* ('palmate') but this may not be well developed, especially in young animals. Never more than two tines on lower half.

Sika: faintly spotted in summer, dark and unspotted in winter; rump white, partially outlined in black, tail shorter than in fallow, *white or faintly streaked with grey;* antlers not distinguishable from those of a young red deer but never more than two tines on basal half and rarely more than four points altogether. A prominent white glandular area on the outside of each hind leg (similar but less conspicuous areas in red and fallow). (Hybridization between sika and red deer has occurred in some areas, e.g. in southern Ireland and in Lancashire.)

Roe: unspotted rich orange-brown in summer, grey-brown in winter; rump white, *no visible tail;* antlers rugose, no more than three points.

Muntjac: very small, with rounded back; unspotted, yellowish or greyish brown; rump white, tail long and dark; *antlers pointing backwards* forming straight line with muzzle, usually only two points, male with tusk-like upper canines.

Water deer: small, light yellowish brown, unspotted; rump white, tail short and dark; *no antlers,* long tusks (upper canines) especially prominent in males; *ears very rounded.*

Wild goat: very variable in colour but no distinctive pale rump; horns very variable in shape but never branched and usually present in both sexes.

Red deer

Fallow

Sika

Roe

Skulls of ungulates, if picked up, may be of wild or domestic species and therefore both are included in the key below. As a group, skulls of ruminants (deer, goat, sheep, ox) are characterized by lack of upper incisors, six cheek teeth in each row with sharply ridged surfaces, apparently four pairs of lower incisors (really three incisors and an incisiform canine) separated by a long gap from the cheek teeth. Skulls of horse and pig are individually distinctive as illustrated.

Skulls with horns (permanent, unbranched bony outgrowths covered with horny sheaths, which may be lost).

1	Horns at extreme back of skull; profile of forehead straight or convex	Ox
	Horns close behind orbits, skull projecting behind the horns; profile of forehead concave	See 2
2	Rounded concavity (lachrymal pit) in front of each orbit	Sheep
	No lachrymal pits	Goat

Skulls without horns (may have antlers which are usually branched, have no sheaths, are shed and renewed annually and grow from persistent bony knobs or pedicles which are blunt, not pointed like small horn-cores).

1	Deep depression (lachrymal pit) in front of each orbit (not to be confused with the actual opening in the skull above the lachrymal pit)	See 2
	No lachrymal pits; (usually no canines; total length of skulls with six pairs of cheek-teeth 150–200mm) ..	Roe
2	Canines absent; (lachrymal pits elongate)	Fallow
	Canines present	See 3
3	Lachrymal pits round, over half the diameter of the orbits; prominent straight ridges above the lachrymal pits and orbits, forming a wide depression on top of the skull; (upper canine large and tusk-like in males)	Muntjac
	Lachrymal pits elongate, under half the diameter of the orbits; no ridges as above	See 4
4	Lachrymal pits small, deep and slit-like; total length not over 200mm; (may have large tusks but never antlers)	Water deer
	Lachrymal pits shallow; total length up to 400mm ..	See 5
5	Lachrymal pits smaller; upper cheek-teeth (if all six present) under 80mm; total length under 300mm ..	Sika
	Lachrymal pits larger; upper cheek-teeth over 80mm; total length up to 400mm	Red deer
	(In the absence of well-developed antlers these species are not easily distinguished without comparison).	

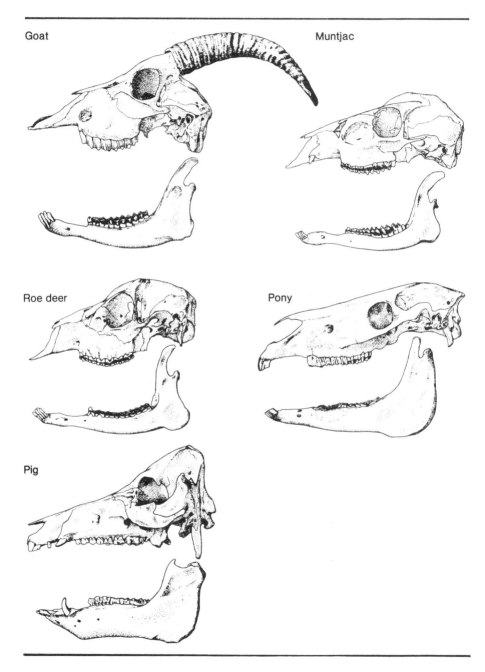

Goat

Muntjac

Roe deer

Pony

Pig

Organizing our information

Having found and identified mammals, what next? Some may wish to pursue their study in greater depth purely for their own enjoyment. But many will want to make their information more generally available. A single record of a weasel in a particular reed-bed on a particular day does not amount to a scientific statement. But if that record is considered along with a sufficient number of others for some generalization to be made about the habitat or distribution of weasels, then these generalizations are indeed scientific statements. As such they can be used to predict the presence of weasels, the accuracy of the prediction depending upon how representative the original observations were.

Our entire knowledge of the fauna and flora of Britain depends upon generalizations of this kind. For one thing we cannot record every animal (although we can get close to that situation with some populations of seals and deer). So we must depend upon samples to predict the overall situation. Time is another complicating factor. Even if we reckon to have made a very thorough study of the distribution of a particular species last year, that does not give us any absolute knowledge of what the status of the species is now – it only allows us to make certain estimates that will be more or less correct depending upon the quality of the facts on which they are based.

In short, individual records must be organized to be meaningful. This organization can be at a strictly local level, for example to record the fauna of a local nature reserve or of a city park, or at a national level. Some ways in which this kind of information is being organized, or could be organized, at these various levels is given below.

Local recording

Many organizations are at present involved in collecting and co-ordinating records of mammals, and other elements of the fauna, on a local or regional basis. These include museums, local natural history societies and county naturalists' trusts. The last are primarily concerned with the conservation of a variety of habitats and now cover the entire country. Many such organizations are conducting surveys with a view to preparing distribution maps for an area such as a county. Most such surveys use as a basis for mapping either the 1km squares of the National Grid (the smallest grid squares shown on 'one inch' and '2$\frac{1}{2}$ inch' maps of the Ordnance Survey), or more often *tetrads* which are 2 × 2km squares. The organisers of such surveys usually welcome either casual records or offers to survey particular areas, and will provide detailed instructions for doing so.

At the more strictly local level recording by grid squares becomes less meaningful and a more useful statement of distribution can be obtained by using actual areas of relatively uniform habitat as the recording units for preparing maps. These areas could for example be a block of suburban houses and gardens surrounded by streets; a wood; a hedgerow; a segment of river bank; or a single field. The optimum size of these units and the boundaries used to define them would vary according to the powers of dispersal of the species concerned.

The mapping of the distribution of mammals is a very suitable project that school classes can sometimes undertake on their own grounds or in an adjacent area such as a park. At this scale we are approaching the size of area that may represent the range of activity of individual animals. In such a case recording presence or absence is less meaningful and a useful approach is to try to get some measure of the amount of utilization of each habitat segment by each species of mammal. But even if this quantitative approach is followed it is better to use as the basic unit an area of similar habitat, such as playing field, long grass, shrubbery, woodland, rather than to use any kind of grid.

National recording

Since 1965 the Mammal Society, in conjunction with the Biological Records Centre, has been collecting records to prepare maps showing the distribution of all mammals in Britain and Ireland. These maps show the presence or absence of a species in 10km squares of the National Grid. A very provisional set of maps was published in 1971, covering Britain and Ireland, and a further set for Ireland only appeared in 1974 (see p. 54: Corbet and Crighton). These projects are continuing. Wherever there is a local recording scheme, say at a county level, it is best if records are submitted to the local recorder who will then forward new records to the national scheme. But in the absence of a local recorder who is collaborating in this way, records may be submitted directly to the Biological Records Centre. They should, however, be entered on recording cards which are obtainable, along with an explanatory leaflet, from:

Biological Records Centre
Monks Wood Experimental Station
Abbots Ripton
Huntingdon PE17 2LS

Fox Bottom: Common seal

Top: Sika deer　Bottom: Grey squirrel

Top: Common shrew   Bottom: Water shrew

Top: Bank vole   Bottom: Field vole

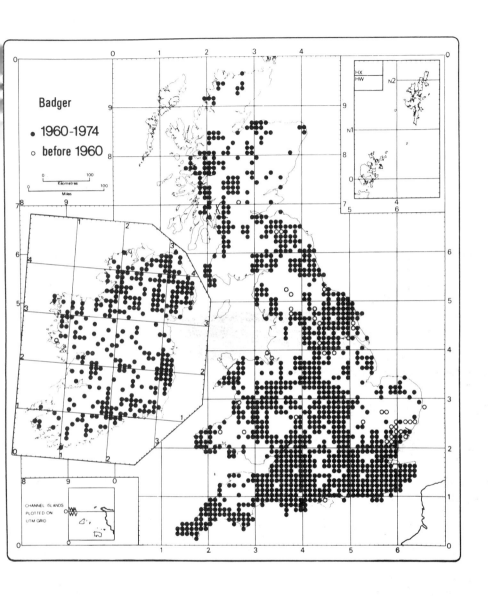

Badger

● 1960-1974
○ before 1960

Map of badger produced by Biological Records Centre

Literature

The following books are of particular value in supplementing the information given here. Most are available in the reference department of many of the larger public libraries.

Anon. 1968. Instructions for collectors no. 1 : mammals (non-marine)
London : British Museum (Nat. Hist.).
Advice on the collecting and preservation of specimens for study (but not taxidermy).

Bang, P and Dahlstrom, P 1974. Collins guide to animal tracks and signs.
London : Collins.

Bateman, J 1971. Animal traps and trapping.
Newton Abbot : David & Charles.
Includes many ideas for home-made traps.

Corbet, G B 1971. Provisional distribution maps of British mammals.
Mammal Review vol. 1, pp. 95–142.
Distribution of all species in Britain and Ireland by 10km grid squares, but very incomplete.

Crighton, M No date. Provisional distribution maps of amphibians, reptiles and mammals in Ireland.
Dublin : Folens & Co.

Fraser, F C 1969. British whales, dolphins and porpoises, 4th ed.
London : British Museum (Nat. Hist.).
Includes illustrations of all species.

Lawrence, M J & Brown, R W 1973. Mammals of Britain : their tracks, trails and signs.
London : Blandford.
Colour photos of most species, drawings of skulls and of many other bones.

Matthews, L H 1952. British mammals.
London : Collins.
A general account with much background biology.

Page, F J T 1971. Field guide to British deer, 2nd ed.
Oxford : Blackwell.
A very practical short guide to the study of deer.

Southern, H N 1964. The handbook of British mammals.
Oxford : Blackwell.
A comprehensive reference work with chapters on techniques of study as well as a systematic account of species. (Out of print – new edition to appear 1976.)

Van Den Brink, F H 1967. A field guide to mammals of Britain and Europe.
London : Collins.
Coloured illustrations.

Index

Muntjac 9, 47-50
Mus 8
Muscardinus 8
Mustela 8
Myocastor 8
Myotis 6, 7, 10

Nathusius' pipistrelle 7, 10, 44, 46
Natterer's bat 6, 44-46
Neomys 6
Noctule 7, 44-46
Nutria = coypu 8, 31
Nyctalus 7

Odobenus 9
Orkney vole 7, 28
Oryctolagus 7
Otter 8, 14, 36, 37, 39

Pagophilus 9
Parti-coloured bat 7, 44, 46
Phoca 9
Pig 50
Pine marten 8, 35
Pinnipedes 9, 40
Pipistrelle 7, 44, 46
Pipistrellus 7
Plecotus 7
Polecat 8, 35, 37, 38
Putorius = *Mustela* 8
Pygmy shrew 6, 12, 24

Rabbit 7, 14, 32
Rats 8, 31
Rattus 8
Red deer 9, 47-49
Red-necked wallaby 6, 33
Red squirrel 7, 30
Rhinolophus 6
Ringed seal 9, 41
Rodents 7, 8, 26, 30
Roe deer 9, 14, 47-50

Scilly shrew =
    lesser white-toothed shrew 6, 25
Sciurus 7
Seals 9, 40
Serotine 7, 44-46
Sheep (skull) 49
Ship rat 8, 31
Short-tailed field mouse =
    field vole 7, 28

Short-tailed vole = field vole 7, 28
Shrews 6, 12, 23-25
Sika 9, 47-49
Skomer vole = bank vole 7, 28
Sorex 6
Squirrels 7, 14, 30
Stoat 8, 34, 37, 38

Talpa 6

Ungulates 47-50

Varying hare = mountain hare 7, 32
Vespertilio 7
Vespertilionid bats 42
Voles 7, 26, 28
Vulpes 8

Wallaby 6, 33
Walrus 9, 41
Water bat 7, 44-46
Water deer 9, 47-49
Water rat 11
Water shrew 6, 18, 24
Water vole 7, 11, 31
Weasel 8, 34, 37, 38
Whiskered bat 6, 10, 44, 46
White-toothed shrews 6, 25
Wild cat 8, 36, 37, 39
Wild goat 47, 49-50
Wood mouse 8, 26, 27

Yellow-necked mouse 8, 27